Outskirts Press, Inc.
http://www.outskirtspress.com

ISBN: 978-1-9772-1467-6

Cover Photo © 2020 Denise Bootsma. All rights reserved - used with permission.

Outskirts Press and the "OP" logo are trademarks belonging to Outskirts Press, Inc.

PRINTED IN THE UNITED STATES OF AMERICA

This Book Belongs to:

_____

From the moment you start to walk up the stairs

The sweet aroma of candy canes fills the air

It really is amazing what we can do

What we can do with the white and the red

What we can do with the red and the white

It really is an amazing sight

Into the kitchen you walk with a grin

Because you know it's about to begin

We greet you with a smile and

welcome you to our show

As the pots been on the fire boiling really really slow

It boils for about twenty minutes or so

Before we add something secret

Drip drop drip and in it goes

A secret ingredient

So secret that we can not say

We cannot say what the secret ingredient is

We would if we could

We could if we may

We may if we could

But we can't and we shan't

As we pour from the hot pot

It's hot hot hot

Don't touch it we say

Please please do not

We scrape and we turn and we flip and we flop

The mixture to cool so we can...

Hook and we hook

Where we pull and we pull

We pull and we stretch

We stretch and we pull

We pull and we stretch

Until the white part is white

Until the white part is as bright

As the white part can be

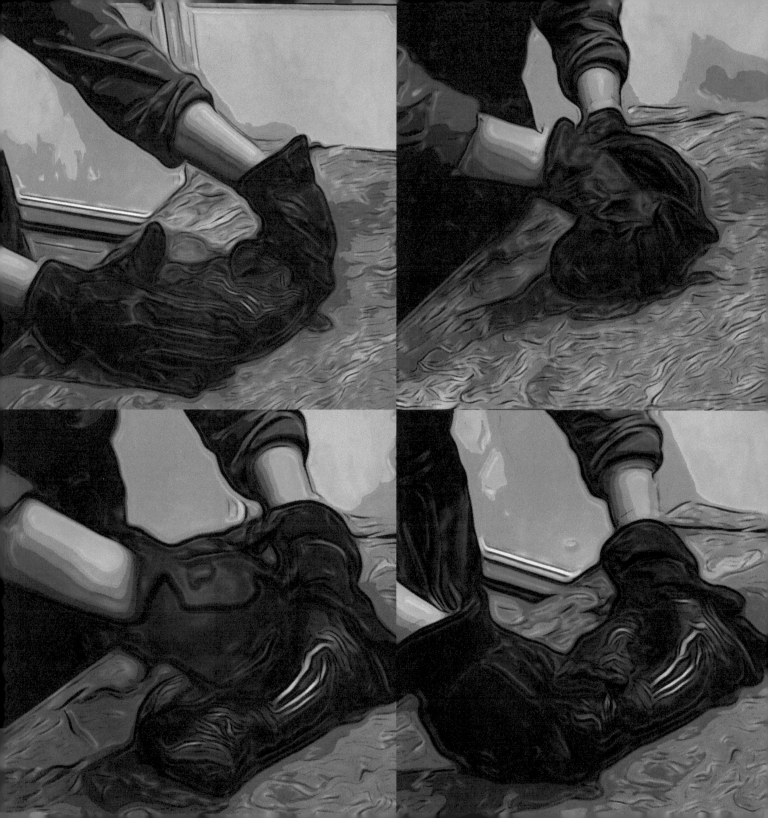

While we turn the white part white

As bright white as can be

We have to add red to make red

So drip drop drip goes the red

And squish, squash, squeeze

Until the red part is as red

As the red part that we need

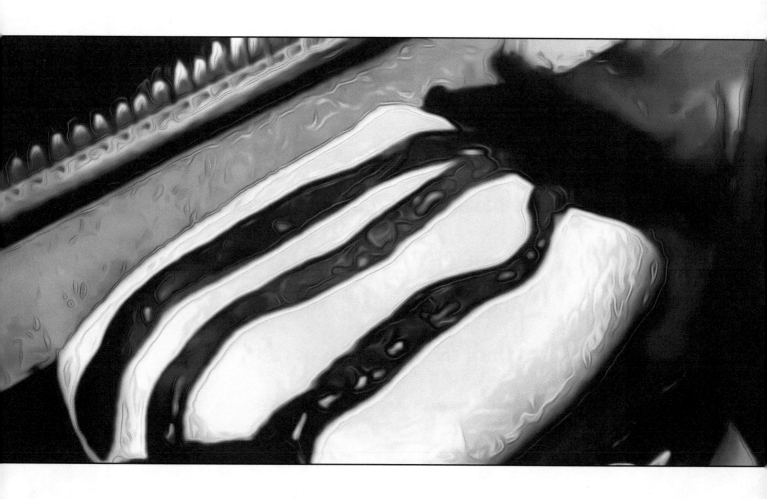

With the bright white part on

top of the red we need part

We move on to the next part

The next part, the striped part

The striped part, all three

We pull and we twist, we twist and we pull

Until they're just right

The white with the red

The red with the white

The white with the red

What a magical sight

Shaping the cane is the last thing we do

With a stretch and a pull

And a pull and a stretch

We pull to the mark

Where we cut and we bend

We bend and we hook

Until LOOK...

The white with the red

The red with the white

A truly magical sight

A sweet striped delight

A bit of history of the candy cane...

It's been said that the candy cane originated in 1670. A choirmaster made white sugar sticks for his young choirboys to help keep them quiet during the scene of Jesus' birth at the Cologne Cathedral in Germany. The church didn't approve of the kids eating candy in church so the choral master added the hook and said that it represented the shepherd's crook and if the cane was upside down, it represented a 'J' for Jesus. The red stripes were said to be added in the 17th century, to represent the blood of Jesus.

Written by Denise Bootsma

2/4/19